Diary of a Unicorn

Also by Connor Hoover

Diary of a Unicorn Series
The Missing Rainbow
The Grumpy Ogre
The Moon Scroll
A Unicorn Christmas

Pick Your Own Quest Series
King Tut's Adventure
Escape From Minecraft
Return to Minecraft
Minecraft The End
Trapped in A Fairy Tale
Dragon vs. Unicorn
Alice in Wonderland
Trapped in the 80s
Medusa's Head

Wizards of Tomorrow Series
Alien Treasure Hunters Series

Diary of a Unicorn

Book 4

A Unicorn Christmas

by
Connor Hoover

ROOTS IN MYTH, AUSTIN, TX

A Unicorn Christmas
Diary of a Unicorn: Book 4

Copyright © 2020 by Connor Hoover.
All rights reserved.
Images from FreePix
Fonts from FontDiner.com, Creative Fabrica, Adobe

All rights reserved. This book may not be reproduced in any manner whatsoever without express permission of the copyright holder.

A Root in Myth Book
Austin, Texas
For more information, write
connor@connorhoover.com

www.connorhoover.com

Paperback ISBN: 978-1-949717-21-1

Merry Christmas, Unicorn Friends!

DATE: GLITTERDAY, EMERALD 12

Happy Holidays, diary!

Shiny Fluffy Hooves here, and I'm sorry I haven't written in a while. I've been busy with so many things. Like first, there was the Clover Festival two weeks ago. I wanted to make Clover cookies for the occasion, but Pumpkin Spice, one of Glitterville's chief bakers, wouldn't let me in the kitchen. She insisted I'd burn the cookies.

BURN THE COOKIES!

I would totally not burn the cookies, but I never got the chance to prove that. Instead, she sent me out to the clover fields to gather only the four-leaf clovers. Pumpkin Spice insisted they made the best cookies. I wasn't really sure how the number of leaves on a clover could have anything to do with the taste of a cookie, but my best friend Star Glitter Tail and I went out to the clover field to find some.

Okay, we got a little distracted.

Also, do you have any idea how hard it is to find four-leaf clovers? I even brought my lucky rock along to help, and we still only ended up with eight.

No, Pumpkin Spice was not happy.

I tried to point out that eight four-leaf clovers was thirty-two leaves, hoping she'd be impressed with my math skills.

She wasn't.

She said she didn't need my help anymore. She made the cookies without me. But the clover festival was still AMAZING! The cookies were so good they melted in my mouth. (I hated to admit this.)

I was all set to write about the festival that night, but then I got invited to a star-watching party for two nights later, and I had to spend all my spare time getting ready for that. A unicorn can't simply show up to a star watching party without knowing all the star patterns. Sure, I knew Princess Honey, the brave unicorn with the bow and arrow. But every unicorn knew that constellation. The three stars in a row made it the easiest to find.

So I hurried to the archives, and I read as many scrolls on star patterns as possible. I figured I had to know at least five.

Right, so I showed up at the star-watching party prepared to show off my star pattern knowledge. But get this! Sassy Mane, of all unicorns, had already pointed out the five I knew. She said they were "basic" and that every unicorn knew them. I had no idea that was the case, but if Sassy Mane knew them, then I figured it must be true. She'd never acted especially interested in constellations or stars before.

Anyway, I didn't look like a rock star at the star-watching party. Still, there were star pies filled with honey, which were amazing. I ate five: one for each of the constellations I knew.

A couple days later was the . . .

Okay, the point I'm trying to make here is that I've been busy, which is why I've missed a couple weeks of writing in you, diary. But don't worry. I'm writing today because I got the most amazing idea ever in the entire world.

Do you want to hear it?

OF COURSE YOU DO!

So as you know (because I put the date at the top of each entry), it's the month of Emerald! And the month of Emerald means Christmas is almost here! Unicorns in Glitterville make a huge deal about Christmas. There are decorations all over town. A giant tree is brought in and placed right by the main glitter fountain. There's singing and dancing and magic. And I thought . . .

*SIDE NOTE: If you think this is a horrible idea, please don't tell me because I'm really excited.

I THOUGHT I WOULD HAVE MY VERY OWN CHRISTMAS PARTY THIS YEAR!

I know! Great idea, right?

A PARTY!

I can already imagine it in my head. I'll invite all the unicorns I know, and there can be a Secret Santa gift exchange. I'll make cookies (in my own kitchen! I don't need to use Pumpkin Spice's kitchen, and I will not burn the cookies.).

We can play games and music and tell stories. And I'm pretty sure it's going to be the most amazing unicorn Christmas party in the entire world.

I told Star about it, and she thinks it's a great idea. Tomorrow I figure I'll tell my mare about it.

What I mean is that I'll ask my mare if it's okay. I'm sure she'll say yes (I hope). I'll make a list and show her how organized I'm going to be on my party planning. And then I'll get started on the invitations.

This is going to be the best unicorn Christmas party ever!

DATE: RAINBOWDAY, EMERALD 13

Right, so I asked my mare. And guess what?

SHE SAID YES!

Well, technically she said I had to promise to not make a mess and to not try any magic in the house.

"Not even for the star on top of the tree?" I asked. Unicorns always used magic to put stars on top of their Christmas trees.

"No magic," my mare said.

I thought about trying to change her mind, but then I got started thinking about the invitations and who all I would invite, and I figured the "no magic" thing was fine.

Also, she might change her mind when the time came.

Star Glitter Tail was really artistic, so I asked her to help me make invitations. She had the great idea to add a cute unicorn doodle, which I love. And we spent the entire morning drawing and coloring them in.

*SIDE NOTE: It takes a lot of time to color in that many invitations!

I think they look amazing. Then we cut up little pieces of paper and wrote every unicorn's name on them for the Secret Santa gift exchange.

Oh, and before you think I was only inviting unicorns, I invited Bruno the Guardian of Maps, the gargoyle that lived in the basement of the archives. He was my friend, too.

I also made an invitation for Razz, better known as Razzlehoff the Destroyer of Temples and the Collector of Kittens. He was my dragon friend. I hadn't figured out how to get the invitation to him just yet, but something would come to mind.

Oh, and then there was Rotgus and Bundek, my dwarf friends. I'd invite them, too.

I thought about inviting Fin Silverbow and Ari Quicksilver, my elf friends (acquaintances?), but since elves couldn't stand dwarves, I decided I'd invite the elves to something else.

Maybe a Spring Solstice party or something like that.

Star and I mixed up the little pieces of paper and put them all in a big bowl. Then we put one piece of paper in each invitation, making sure nobody got themselves. It's hard to get yourself a present. I mean, technically it's easy because you always know what you want.

Or maybe you don't always know what you want. Sometimes the best gifts are the ones you never knew you needed in your life. Like the time Star gave me a star-light for my room. When I turned it on, little spots of light lit up the entire ceiling and walls. And then there was the gift that . . .

WAIT! I'M GETTING OFF TRACK.

The whole point is that nobody got their own name.

"Who did you get?" I asked Star.

She looked at her little piece of paper. "Sweet Cupcakes," Star said.

Sweet Cupcakes was the head archivist at the archives.

"Who'd you get?" Star asked.

I looked at my paper. Oh no!!!

SASSY MANE!?!?

I showed Star the piece of paper, and she started giggling. Then I started giggling, too.

See, Sassy Mane didn't really like me. I wasn't sure why. I was such an agreeable, nice unicorn. I think—okay, and this is very hard for me to admit—I think she thought I wasn't cool enough to be her friend.

NOT COOL ENOUGH!

I'd done all sorts of cool things. I'd found a missing rainbow. I'd gotten rid of a horrible ogre. But you know what? Not only was I going to throw the most amazing unicorn Christmas party, I was going to find Sassy Mane the best Secret Santa gift ever!

No, I had no idea what that was going to be. But I had a week. I'd figure something out.

* * *

Star had play practice in the afternoon. See, every year in Glitterville, for Christmas, there is this amazing unicorn play. Sometimes it's scary, like one year the play was about ogres stealing our Glitterville Christmas tree. (Lots of unicorns complained about that one.) Sometimes it's happy, like sharing presents with all sorts of creatures in the woods.

Star wasn't allowed to tell me what the play was about this year. The theatre group always kept it secret. But from the way she was talking, I think it had something to do with decorating a Christmas tree.

Which reminded me, I'd have to find a tree tomorrow for my house! I couldn't have a Christmas party without a Christmas tree. And then once I found the tree, I had to decorate it. And then I had to . . .

THERE WAS SO MUCH WORK TO DO!

I took a deep breath. Everything was going to be okay. I had time to get everything done.

I HOPED!

I stopped by the school first. Mr. Canter, our science and magic teacher, was there along with five other unicorns. Thankfully they were all in my class, so they were all invited.

Oh, what if I forgot to invite some unicorn? I wished I could invite every unicorn in Glitterville, but my mare specifically said that

I couldn't. She said, "Shiny, you can't invite every unicorn in Glitterville." Those were her exact words.

"I'm having a party," I said, and I passed out the invitations.

"Oh, I love parties," Cinnamon Sparkles said. "Especially Christmas parties!" Then she tossed her red sparkly mane over her shoulders. It was so pretty.

*SIDE NOTE: My mane was really pretty, too! No, I'm not trying to brag. But ever since the awful "magic disaster" it had been frizzy and brittle. But I'd fixed it! Sure, I nearly got electrocuted while doing so, but I didn't want to dwell on that part of the story.

I tossed my purple mane over my shoulders, too.

Racer Diamonds looked at the invitation with wide eyes. "Will Star Glitter Tail be there?" he asked. He had a huge crush on Star. Which reminded me, I should really hang mistletoe in my house for the party. I had dreams of . . .

Never mind.

"Of course!" I said. "And I hope you all can make it, too."

I stopped by the archives and delivered invitations to Sweet Cupcakes, Bruno, and even Old Gray Stars, the ancient unicorn who lived on the top floor of the archives. He was asleep when I got there, but I left it on the table where his head rested. I hoped he wouldn't drool on it.

I found a couple of raccoons near one of the trees in Glitterville and asked if they'd be willing to deliver my invitations to Razz, Rotgus, and Bundek. The raccoons were a little skeptical at first, but I promised them some cookies if they did it. That was all it took. They each grabbed an invitation and scurried off over the walls of Glitterville, invitations clutched in their claws. Hopefully they wouldn't eat the invitations!

I made a few more stops, and with each one, I was happier. This really was the best idea ever! Every unicorn was so excited about the party. They especially liked the idea of the Secret Santa gift exchange. Then I stopped by Sassy Mane's house.

Her mare answered the door, and I held up the invitation. "I'm having a party!" I said.

What in the world was I going to get Sassy Mane as a present?

"Sassy!" her mare called. "Shiny is here!"

I mentioned that Sassy Mane didn't really like me. Yeah, well, I seriously heard her groan from the other room. Then she said, "Can you tell her I'm busy putting my makeup on?"

OF COURSE SHE WAS!

"Sassy Mane, you get out here right now!" her mare said.

Thirty seconds later Sassy Mane pranced into the room. "Oh, hi, Shiny. Did you forget to brush your mane today?"

I gritted my teeth together and held out the invitation. Even if Sassy Mane didn't like me, I could still be nice to her . . . even if she made me want to SCREAM sometimes!

"I'm having a Christmas party," I said. "And you're invited."

"Oh," Sassy Mane said. "I'll have to check my calendar."

But then her mare stepped in. "Nonsense. I already put it on your calendar."

See, my mare and Sassy Mane's mare were good friends.

Sassy Mane pretended to smile really big. "Well, then I guess I'll be there."

"Have you found a tree yet, Shiny?" her mare asked.

I shook my head. "I'm doing that tomorrow."

Sassy Mane's mare clapped her front hooves together. "Perfect! Sassy can go with you!"

Sassy Mane and I both looked at each other. I'm sure my mouth dropped open. I had no idea what to say. I didn't want Sassy Mane tree hunting with me, and I couldn't imagine that she wanted to go either.

I guess her mare took our silence to mean we were both cool with it.

"Perfect," her mare said. "Sassy will be ready in the morning."

After they closed the door behind me, it took me a solid five minutes to refocus. I sat on the edge of one of the smaller glitter fountains in Glitterville. It would be fine. And it's hard for me to admit, but somewhere in my mind, I imagined Sassy Mane and me actually becoming friends. Maybe her coming along with me would make that happen.

Not that I wanted Sassy Mane to be my friend. I mean, I didn't want her to not be my friend. Ugh, why was this so complicated?

"I hear you're having a party," some unicorn said.

I looked up to see Dashing Hearts looking right at me.

DASHING HEARTS!

Okay, a moment here. Dashing Hearts was the best-looking unicorn in Glitterville . . . at least I thought so. He had this amazing light blue hair and a dark blue mane and hooves. But the most amazing thing was his red horn and the matching red hearts all over his hair.

Yes, I totally had a crush on him.

Yes, I totally imagined kissing him under the mistletoe.

"Um...," I stammered. "A party?"

He gave me a smile that seriously made my heart flop upside-down. "Yes, a party. For Christmas. You're having one?"

HE WAS TALKING TO ME. ABOUT MY PARTY!!!

I gulped and tried to pull myself together. I was prepared for this.

"Right," I said. "I am having a party. And I have an invitation for you."

See, I was prepared!

Dashing Hearts held out a hoof, and I passed him the invitation. This was like unicorn magic because I'd been so scared to deliver the invitation to his house, and yet here he was!

"I can't wait," Dashing Hearts said.

HE COULDN'T WAIT!

"Do you have a tree yet?" he asked.

I shook my head, hoping Sassy Mane was wrong and that my purple mane looked shiny and silky as it tossed side to side. "No yet. But I'm going tomorrow to get one."

Dashing Hearts seemed to think about this for a second. Then he said, "I could come along with you if you want."

OMG! This was like a dream come true.

Except wait. Sassy Mane was coming also.

"That would be—" I started.

"Perfect," Dashing Hearts said. "I'll see you first thing in the morning."

I don't really remember delivering the rest of the invitations. All I could think about was tomorrow. It was going to be the most amazing day ever!

DATE: SPARKLEDAY, EMERALD 14

It was not the most amazing day ever.

Let me start by saying that hunting for a Christmas tree did not turn out like I expected. Like if I could have imagined how the day would go, it would be something like this: Me, Sassy Mane, and Dashing Hearts would head outside the gates of Glitterville.

Wait, scratch that. Let me start over.

Me and Dashing Hearts would head outside the gates of Glitterville. Sassy Mane wouldn't be able to go because of a . . . HAIR DISASTER! Yes, her aqua blue and white mane maybe would go completely frizzy, and she'd have to spend the day taking care of that, making it impossible for her to go with us.

So sad.

Anyway, me and Dashing Hearts would wander out into the forest. We'd find the perfect tree. And just before we got back to Glitterville with the tree, Dashing Hearts would tell me how I was the most amazing and smartest unicorn in the world.

Do you have that image in your head?

Okay, good. Now completely erase it, because that is not how things went even kind of sort of. Let's get back to reality.

So I walked outside my house, making sure to bring some snacks I'd made the night before. I'd stayed up late baking cookies, and yes, they were slightly burned on the bottom. I'd tried to scrape that part off. Also, I'd iced them a bit too early, so they were all sticking together. They were more like an iced cookie ball. But whatever.

I waited by the main glitter fountain, which, since it was Sparkleday, was swirling and sparkling in the morning sunrise. Some unicorn must have done some magic this morning because the colors were changing from red to green to blue and all the colors of the rainbow.

It was mesmerizing. I couldn't pull my eyes away.

"Shiny?" someone said.

I whipped my head around, nearly cracking my neck. There was Dashing Hearts. His head was held high, and the morning sun, like with the fountain, was making his red horn and hearts sparkle. I never realized it before, but there was actually glitter in the red color.

"Oh, uh, hi," I managed to say, trying to ignore the shooting pain that had moved from my neck through my entire body.

"How do I look this morning?" he asked.

How did he look? It was a bit of a strange question, but he did look amazing, and since he asked, I might as well tell him so.

"You look . . ." Wait. I didn't want to tell him he looked amazing. That sounded so ushy gushy. "Fine?"

His face froze. "Fine? That's it?"

Sassy Mane walked up right then. No, her mane was not frizzy from any hair disaster.

"You look sparkly and magical," Sassy Mane said to Dashing Hearts.

His mouth spread into a wide grin. "Perfect. Now let's go find Shiny a Christmas tree."

The three of us headed outside the gates of Glitterville. And even though my neck was starting to feel a lot better, I was a little concerned for Sassy Mane and Dashing Hearts. They seemed to be having some kind of silent competition on who could toss their mane better over their shoulders. That's the kind of thing that could give a unicorn whiplash.

We wandered into the forest, and given that it was a beautiful sparkly day and we were three unicorns, all sorts of cute creatures stopped to chat with us. There was the bunny family I always ran into, some squirrels trying to collect nuts for the winter. A couple of mamma deer and their babies. The babies were so cute! (Baby deer are called fawns in case you didn't know.) Then a porcupine wandered across our path.

"What are three unicorns doing out here?" the porcupine said. "Didn't you hear about the danger?"

"Danger?" Sassy Mane said, and she looked to me.

LIKE I COULD DO SOMETHING ABOUT IT!

"What kind of danger?" I asked.

The porcupine lowered his voice, like he didn't want any other creatures to hear. "Wolves. A pack of four of them."

WOLVES!

I'd met some wolves in Goldcrest, a town up north that I'd visited, and yes, I was sure they were going to eat me. The only reason they didn't was because I was with the dragon, Razz, at the time. But Razz wasn't here now.

Dashing Hearts stepped forward and held his head high. "Don't worry," he said. "I'll protect us from any dangers we may come across. Now off with you, silly porcupine."

Off with you? What was that about?

But the porcupine didn't look offended. He just shrugged, cast a couple sharp quills on the ground, and wandered off.

Dashing Hearts turned to me and Sassy Mane. "I'm not scared of anything," he said.

And even though it should have made me feel better, he wasn't all that convincing.

We kept wandering deeper and deeper into the forest. Yes, we saw lots of trees, but none of them were just right. Like one tree that Dashing Hearts picked out wasn't nearly fluffy enough (Sassy Mane's words). And another one that Sassy Mane suggested was vertically challenged (it was about half my height, so those were my words). And another one . . .

Okay, you get the idea. We hadn't found the perfect tree yet.

"Can't we just agree on the next one we see and head back?" Sassy finally asked when we stopped for snacks.

"No way! I want the tree to be perfect." I held a hoof up over my head. "It should be this tall and fluffy with fresh needles and no dying branches." I pulled out my cookie ball to share. By now it was one big glop. "Cookies?"

Sassy Mane seemed to consider the cookie ball, then lifted her upper lip into a sneer. "Ew, gross."

"Whatever." I took a bite. They may not look the best, but they tasted great.

"Fine. I'll find us the perfect tree," Sassy said. "From this point forward, I'm now in charge. Now let's get back to it."

Was this any different than normal? Sassy Mane always acted like she was in charge anyway.

But Dashing Hearts said, "Oh, I was hoping we could take a nap. You know, beauty sleep is very important."

Both Sassy Mane and I turned to look at him. Her mouth dropped open, and I'm pretty sure mine did, too.

"Beauty sleep?" I said.

He let out a small laugh. "Well, of course. You don't think it's easy looking this good, do you?"

Whoa. Can you say "overly concerned about looks?"

"Do you take beauty naps every day?" I asked. I had way too many things I wanted to do each day to take naps.

He brushed at his silky blue mane with a hoof, straightening a couple stray hairs. "Pretty much."

Sassy Mane stood up. "Well, you're going to have to skip your beauty nap today. Let's go."

"But . . . ," Dashing Hearts started.

"I'm in charge," Sassy Mane said. "Now get up!"

Way to go, Sassy Mane! Still, Dashing Hearts was pretty dreamy, and I didn't want him to get upset.

"Maybe you can take a nap later," I said. "Under the perfect Christmas tree."

"Maybe," Dashing Hearts said.

We set back out, and then we came to a fork in the path. To the right, the sun was shining, and the grass was the same color green as emeralds. To the left, the trees were thick, blocking out a lot of the sun. The grass was more like moss that had grown over the rocky path. Moss wasn't all that tasty. The choice seemed pretty obvious.

Dashing Hearts turned to the path on the right.

"Wrong way," Sassy Mane said.

WRONG WAY? WHAT?

"But it's dark and scary down that path," Dashing Hearts said.

Hmmm . . .

"Scary?" I said. "I thought you weren't scared of anything."

He straightened his neck, standing tall. "Well, I'm not. I was just thinking of you two. I know girls can get scared sometimes."

Here's the thing. I can normally think of anything to say in any situation. But WHAT?

Sassy Mane was as speechless as I was. We both just stared at Dashing Mane.

He held his head high and grinned at us. "Am I right?"

"No, you are not right!" I said.

"We are not scared," Sassy Mane said.

Dashing Hearts looked to the left, at the dark path ahead. "But what about what the porcupine said? Wolves have been spotted."

"We're going to be fine," Sassy Mane said. "And since you're so brave, you can lead the way."

Dashing Hearts gulped. "Um . . . I can?" It came out more like a question than any sort of reassurance.

"Unless you're too scared," I said.

Dashing Hearts eyed the dark woods. "I am not too scared. I just don't see why we have to go this way."

"Because there are more trees to the left," Sassy Mane said. "And the sooner I find us the perfect tree, the sooner we can go home."

She made a very good point. Sunshine and green grass weren't going to lead to the best trees. The best trees would be deep in the forest.

WHERE THE WOLVES WERE!

I pushed that thought to the back of my mind.

"Fine." Dashing Hearts stepped to the left, placing one hoof on the path. "But you two need to keep up. I don't want anyone getting lost."

Okay, I'd seen lots of things in the last few months, but the dark woods were still terrifying. Like I completely couldn't see the sun. I could hardly spot the blue of the sky. There were noises, like creatures, but not cute little creatures like bunny rabbits and squirrels. More like wolves and big foots. But I really did want to find the perfect tree.

"There's a break up ahead," Sassy Mane said, pointing with a hoof.

She was right. There was a small spot of grass and . . .

"Water!"

We all hurried ahead. It had been hours since we'd seen any running water, and all this worrying about the dark path was making me thirsty.

We came to a clearing with a small lake in the center. The trees were nowhere near as thick here, and I looked up, finally able to see the blue sky.

Wait a second.

THE SKY WASN'T BLUE!

Dark storm clouds swirled and churned, and the wind picked up, starting to blow through the trees. It howled, like it was alive.

"Do you guys hear the wind?" I asked. My mane was blowing in a million different directions.

"That's not the wind!" Dashing Hearts said. "Those are wolves!"

OH NO! HE WAS RIGHT!

"Run!" Sassy Mane shouted, and the three of us dashed around the lake and back into the thick woods. Sassy Mane skirted around Dashing Hearts and led the way. I never would have believed she could run so fast, but she was at a full gallop. Her mane flew behind her like something out of a fantasy story. I was right there behind her, my hooves pumping on the hard ground. I was pretty sure Dashing Hearts was behind me, but I wasn't about to turn and look.

The howling came from every direction, the sound of the wind mixing with the cry of the wolves. They sounded like they were right behind us. We had to find somewhere to hide.

"In here," Sassy Mane shouted, and she dashed into a small cave cut into the side of a hill.

I didn't stop to consider my options. I hurried in the cave and moved away from the entrance.

"Hurry, Dashing Hearts!" Sassy Mane called.

Dashing Hearts was still way behind us, picking every step carefully through the woods. "I don't want to ruin my hair!" he called back.

"Forget about your hair!" Sassy Mane shouted. "The wolves are coming!"

This seemed enough to remind Dashing Hearts of the looming danger. His hooves hit hard on the ground, kicking up dirt and stones which the wind picked up and swirled around. He stumbled but managed to stay upright. And then he was in the cave.

"Quick, to the back," I said, and the three of us scurried as deep into the cave as we could go while still being able to make sure we weren't about to fall into some pit of doom.

"Don't say a word," Sassy Mane said.

And the three of us sat in silence. I wanted to sneeze about twenty different times, but I didn't dare. Outside the wind still howled. The wolves got closer. Their scent filled the air, blowing into the cave.

WHAT IF THEY COULD SMELL US???

Then they were right outside. I could hear them breathing.

"Where did the unicorns go?" I heard one of them say.

"I don't know," another said. "I lost their scent."

LOST OUR SCENT?

I looked to Sassy Mane who gave a small smile. She must've done some kind of magic to hide our smell.

Then the wolves howled a few more times and ran off, into the storm and the approaching night.

* * *

We waited until we were sure the wolves were long gone. Even though we were protected from the wind in this cave, it was chilly inside.

"Oh, I'll start a fire," Dashing Hearts said.

WHEW! What a relief!

Okay, maybe I spoke too soon. Dashing Hearts gathered some sticks from outside the cave entrance and placed them in a pile. Then he pointed his horn at the sticks.

I'll give him a tiny amount of credit. I did see one spark.

ONE SPARK!

"I'm normally so good at this," Dashing Hearts said.

Normally? How many campfires was he lighting?

"Really?" Sassy Mane asked.

"Oh, totally," Dashing Hearts said. "Maybe you guys are interfering with my magical aura."

Was he trying to say it was our fault he couldn't light the fire?

He tried again. This time there wasn't even a spark.

"Yep, it's definitely because of you two. You must have negative energy."

NEGATIVE ENERGY!

"Whatever," I said. "I'll do it." And I tried. I really tried. I focused every bit of magical energy from my horn toward the pile of sticks. I tried to imagine flames shooting out, like when Razz the dragon spit fire out his nostrils. But there wasn't even a puff of smoke.

"Have you tried yet, Shiny?" Dashing Hearts said. "Because it sure doesn't look like it."

I glared at him.

Sassy Mane stood up and walked to the pile of sticks. "Here, let me try," she said. "There's obviously something blocking magic in this cave."

And what? She thought it wouldn't affect her?

But Sassy Mane didn't point her horn at the sticks. Instead, she picked up two of the larger sticks and started rubbing them together against her hoof. And if I hadn't seen it, I never would have believed it, but first there was smoke, and then a small flame burst to life. She moved the flame to the pile of sticks and lit the whole thing on fire.

"You did it!" I said.

Dashing Hearts mumbled something that sounded like, "Well, I could have done it that way."

I seriously doubted that. I certainly couldn't have done it that way.

"You can't rely on magic for everything," Sassy Mane said. Then she tossed the sticks into the fire.

"But where'd you learn to do that?" I asked. I don't think I'd ever been so impressed by Sassy Mane in my life.

Sassy Mane shrugged. "Camping, I guess. But please don't tell every unicorn back in Glitterville about this."

"Why?" If I had just lit a fire with some sticks, I would want every unicorn to know! I'd want the entire world to know.

Sassy Mane rolled her eyes. The firelight flickering on her eyelashes made them look especially pretty. "It's just not that cool, okay?"

I didn't say anything for at least ten seconds. Then I said, "Well, I think it's pretty cool."

By now it was completely nighttime outside. The wind was finally settling down, but given that there were still wolves out in the forest, I was pretty sure that none of us were going anywhere for the rest of the night.

I pulled my cookie ball out of my bag and held it out. "Cookies?"

Sassy Mane eyed it again, as if it were the hardest decision of her life. Then she finally grabbed it and took a huge bite. Her eyes went wide, and a small smile crept onto her face.

VICTORY! My cookies may look horrible, but they still tasted good.

"Oh, it's really good, Shiny," she said.

What I almost said: "I TOLD YOU SO!"

What I said instead: "Thanks."

I guess this was enough for Dashing Hearts to finally try a bite also. And the three of us sat around the fire and ate the entire cookie ball.

* * *

Fifteen minutes later, Dashing Hearts was curled up and fast asleep. I wasn't tired yet, so I stood up.

"I'm going outside to look at the stars," I said to Sassy Mane. "Do you want to come?"

"Look at stars?" she said. "That's so nerdy." But she stood up and followed me outside the cave.

The storm was gone, and the sky was filled with stars. "There's Princess Honey," I said, pointing to the only constellation I remembered. I'd forgotten the other four.

"She's watching over us," Sassy Mane said. She pointed to the other side of the sky. "And there's her mother, Queen Jasmine. She's not there for half the year, during the spring and summer. She goes to visit King Capricorn, and Princess Honey gets really lonely. But then in the fall and winter, Queen Jasmine comes back and they always celebrate Christmas together."

"Wait, really?" I'd never known about Princess Honey's parents, the king and queen. "Where'd you learn that?"

Sassy Mane glanced down, like she didn't want to look me in the eye. "If I tell you, you have to promise not to tell any other unicorn ever. Do you promise?"

"I guess," I said.

She blew out a long breath. "I really like astronomy and the constellations and stuff. So I go once a week to the top floor of the archives, and this old unicorn that lives up there gives me lessons and lets me look through this giant telescope."

"You mean Old Gray Stars!" I said.

"Yes! But how did you know?"

"Because I know him, too," I said. "And that's so cool. Why wouldn't you want other unicorns to know?"

Sassy Mane finally looked at me. "Because it's not my image, Shiny. I'm into fashion and makeup and jewelry. That's what every unicorn expects of me. They don't expect constellations and stars and stuff like that."

I was really confused. "But shouldn't your image just be who you are?"

"Not if I want to be the most popular unicorn at Glitterville School," Sassy Mane said. "But you wouldn't understand."

She was right. I wouldn't understand, because even though I wanted other unicorns to like me, I didn't want to pretend to not like things that I liked. Or do things that I didn't want to do.

"Well, I think it's very cool that you like astronomy," I said. "Can you point out a few more constellations?"

So we sat there for another hour, under the stars, and Sassy Mane pointed out all the constellations she knew and told me the stories behind them. And I had to admit that if Sassy Mane were like this all the time, I could actually imagine being friends with her.

DATE: FRIENDDAY, EMERALD 15

Here's the problem. Sassy Mane was not like that all the time. The next morning, bright and early, Sassy Mane was up.

"Back at it, unicorns!" she said. "It's time for me to find us the perfect tree."

Dashing Hearts grumbled something. I think he was trying to say that he needed more beauty sleep.

She kneed him. "Get up, lazy!"

I couldn't help but giggle. So far on this trip, neither Sassy Mane nor Dashing Hearts had turned out to be the unicorns I thought they were.

We headed back out into the forest, but the path was a mess. I guess it was from the storm last night. Branches and trees were everywhere, scattered all over the path. We stepped over them as we headed back the way we'd came.

"I'm sure we'll find the perfect tree around here," Sassy Mane said.

"What about this one?" Dashing Hearts said, pointing to the scrawniest tree I'd seen in my life.

"Too small," Sassy Mane said.

"What about this one?" The tree he pointed to next had about ten total pine needles.

"Too thin," I said.

And so this went on, one tree after the next, at least thirty more times.

Finally Dashing Hearts couldn't take it anymore. "Can we please just find a tree and go back to Glitterville? I have an appointment to get my hooves polished this afternoon, and if I miss it, I'll have to wait weeks for another appointment."

"You get your hooves polished?" I asked.

"Well, of course," Dashing Hearts said. "Like I said. It's not easy looking this good."

He did look good. But if his entire life revolved around worrying about his looks, that seemed kind of a waste.

"Why do you care so much about how you look?" I asked.

This question seemed to stump him. "Well . . . I just want to make sure unicorns like me, I guess."

"And you think if you don't look good unicorns won't like you?" I asked.

"Well, I don't know if they'll like me or not," Dashing Hearts said. "But what if they don't? What if I lose all my friends because I don't look good?"

It was the most messed up reasoning I'd ever heard in my life!

"Then they aren't your real friends," I said. "Real friends should like you no matter what you look like. Remember when my mane was frizzy?"

Sassy Mane giggled. "Every unicorn remembers when your mane was frizzy!"

I ignored that.

"Yeah, well, Star, my best friend, she didn't care. That's what a real friend is like. They like you even when you're having bad hair days."

"Or months," Sassy Mane said. "But I agree with Shiny."

SHE DID?

"You do?" I asked.

"Sure," Sassy Mane said. "Your friends should like you no matter what you look like."

"Or what you like to do," I added, referring to her interest in star-watching.

Sassy Mane didn't say a thing.

And we kept walking.

And I was starting to lose hope that we would ever find the perfect tree because we were getting back to where the paths had originally split.

That's when Sassy Mane said, "OMG! Look! The perfect tree!"

She cantered ahead and stopped where a tree had fallen over, blocking the path. Dashing Hearts and I hurried to join her.

"Look at it, Shiny!" Sassy Mane said.

I looked around to see which tree she was talking about, but then she pointed at the ground. And she was right. The pine tree that had fallen on the path was perfect. It was big, but not too big. It had enough needles that you could hardly see the branches. The color was a shade of green like emeralds.

IT WAS PERFECT!

"I love it!" I said.

"Me, too," Sassy said. "And you know the best part? It's already fallen over, so we don't have to cut it down. It will be better for the environment!"

Wait. Sassy Mane cared about stuff like that?

She went on. "This tree was meant to be our Christmas tree . . . I mean your Christmas tree."

Mine. Ours. It didn't matter. This was the tree we were meant to find.

Between the three of us and a small helping of magic, we were able to drag the tree back to Glitterville. Once we were through the gates, Dashing Hearts immediately ran off, reminding us of his hoof-polishing appointment.

"Hoof polishing!" Sassy Mane said. Then we both started giggled.

"You think I should get my hooves polished?" I asked Sassy Mane.

"Maybe we both should," Sassy said. Then she helped me drag the tree the rest of the way to my house and cantered away.

My mare helped me pull the tree inside, and since my mare was amazing at magic, we had it set up in the center of the family room in no time. Okay, sure, finding the tree took a day longer than I expected, but it was worth it. Even my mare agreed. I had the perfect Christmas tree. Now I needed to make sure everything else was perfect for the party.

DATE: STARDAY, EMERALD 16

Star showed up first thing in the morning. When I opened the door, there she was holding two cups in her hooves.

"Unicorn Swirl Frappe?" she said and passed one to me.

I took a huge sip then wiped my mouth because I was pretty sure I had whipped cream all over it. "You are the best friend in the world! And wait until you see my tree!"

She stepped in and immediately spotted the tree. "OMG Shiny, it's perfect! I can't believe you found such a perfect tree."

"Sassy Mane actually found it," I said, and I filled her in on the entire tree-hunting adventure.

"You were stuck in a cave with Sassy Mane and Dashing Hearts?" she said. "How was that?"

The short answer was that neither of them was quite who I thought they were. I wanted to tell Star about how Sassy Mane was actually into astronomy, but I promised that I wouldn't, and no way would I break a promise.

"Not what I would have imagined at all," I said. "Oh, and Sassy Mane knows how to start a fire—without magic!"

That part wasn't a secret.

"Impressive," Star said. "Now weren't we going to find Secret Santa presents today?"

Oh no. That's right. I had to find Sassy Mane some kind of present that she would like.

We finished our frappes, and Star and I headed out to the center of downtown where all the shops were.

Here's how shopping went in Glitterville. Unicorns didn't use money. Okay, at least unicorns in Glitterville didn't use money. Maybe in other unicorn towns, they did use money. And I had no idea what alicorns used to trade. Which reminded me that I still wanted to visit the alicorn town down south someday. But anyway, I'm getting off track.

Here in Glitterville, we don't use money. But we do need things, so yes, there are shops downtown. And if something needs fixed around the house and neither my mare nor I can fix it, we can call another unicorn to come fix it for us. We don't pay with money. Instead we trade.

There are lots of things to trade, when you really think about it. Small treats to eat, bags of fresh clover, magic, songs, the promise of making cakes. The list could really go on and on. That's what I never understood about the whole money thing. There was no creativity in buying stuff with money.

Anyway, you get the idea.

Star and I walked into this really hip shop on the corner of the main street called Spices. We'd been trying for forever to figure out what the name meant. Maybe once upon a time they sold spices. Or maybe a unicorn named Spice started it and forgot to put an apostrophe on the name. Or maybe . . .

Well, those were the two best theories we had at this point.

There were three other unicorns in Spices. I immediately went to a glass cabinet where they kept a bunch of jewelry and fancy hair accessories. Sassy Mane would probably love a fancy hair accessory. Except then I remembered that she had about a million fancy hair accessories. She had flowers and rainbows and cupcakes and hearts and pretty much every other design. I know this because she wears a different one every single day.

I was about to walk away from the hair accessories when a sparkly one caught my eye. It was a group of seven gems, all different colors, but they were placed together like . . .

A CONSTELLATION!

This was perfect! I couldn't imagine a more perfect gift for Sassy Mane.

I reached for the hair accessory, but then I stopped. If I got this for her, she might get upset because it might let other unicorns know that she really liked astronomy. But it was perfect for her. Like if I could have imagined a more perfect gift, it would be something that couldn't exist because this was the top of the perfect scale when it came to gifts for Sassy Mane.

You know what? Sassy Mane would love this gift. I knew she would. I was going to take the risk and get it for her.

I met Star halfway to the checkout counter.

"What'd you find?" she asked me.

I help up the hair accessory.

"Ooooh, sparkly!" Star said. "Sassy Mane will love all those colors."

RIGHT?!?!

"What did you find for Sweet Cupcakes?" I asked.

"Oh, wait until you see!" Star reached into her bag and pulled out a scroll.

I was about to point out that Sweet Cupcakes was around thousands of scrolls all day long. But then Star said, "It's magic!"

A MAGIC SCROLL???

How cool was that?

"What kind of magic does it do?" I asked.

The smile slipped a tiny bit from Star's face. "Oh, I'm not sure. I mean I'm sure it's good magic, but I don't know what that magic will do. But I'm sure that Sweet Cupcakes will love it."

Yes, I bet you can guess the thought that went through my mind. Without knowing if the magic was good or not, there was no telling what the scroll was capable of. But Sweet Cupcakes was an archivist. Any scroll (even if it happened to be an evil magic scroll with the power to turn every unicorn in Glitterville into an ogre) was something she'd be interested in.

"She is going to love it!" I said.

"Right!"

It was our turn at the counter. I traded some clover fritters my mare had made, and Star traded a sparkle of magic, good to be used anytime in the next month. Then we walked out of the shop.

Racer Diamonds was just walking in. He tripped over his own hooves when he saw Star.

"Oh, hi, Star," Racer Diamonds said, and even though he was green, I was sure he was blushing under his hair.

"Hi, Racer Diamonds," Star said. "What are you doing?"

He glanced to me. "Picking out something for the Secret Santa gift swap." Then he blushed some more and went inside Spices.

"I bet he's getting you a present," I said to Star.

"Wait. Why?"

I gently tapped her with a hoof. "Because he likes you!"

"He does not."

And we spent the walk back to my place arguing (in a very friendly way) about it. Star had to know Racer Diamonds liked her.

Star and I made some popcorn, covered it with plenty of glitter sprinkles, and got to work decorating the tree. By the time it was dark, the only thing left was placing the star on the top of the tree.

"Want me to do it?" Star asked, preparing to use her magic.

But my mare had said no magic, and I'd been thinking about this. I had it figured out. I was hoping someone else would be putting the star on top of my Christmas tree.

"Not yet," I said. Then I yawned. "Are you coming over to help me make cookies tomorrow?"

Star's eyes went wide. "Cookies! Of cour—oh wait. I can't."

SHE CAN'T?!?! But I needed Star. You remember what happened the last time I made cookies. I ended up with that giant cookie ball. I couldn't have cookie balls for my epic Christmas party.

"Are you sure?" I asked.

Star blew out a long breath. "I have play rehearsal all day," she said. "I'm sorry, Shiny."

I tried not to act too disappointed. "It's fine. I can make cookies on my own."

I hoped.

DATE: SUNNYDAY, EMERALD 17

Here's the short synopsis of my day:
    I could NOT, in fact, make cookies on my own.

Here's the longer version:

My mare left early in the morning to go to work. Which was great. This way, if I made a mess and had a bunch of dishes to wash, she wouldn't get upset at me. If only dishes to wash were my biggest problem. But I'm getting ahead of myself.

I started by printing out six different cookie recipes. After all, you can't have just one kind of Christmas cookie at a Christmas party. I'd make six today and six tomorrow and then the party would be the next day, and that would be twelve different kinds of cookies for all my friends to choose from.

I cleared off enough space on the counters so I could make all six cookies at the same time. I figured that way I'd save lots of time. I placed the printed recipes on the counter, and then I started collecting my ingredients. Flour. Sugar. Eggs. Milk. Except four of the recipes called for flour. And all of them called for sugar. And I was going to need to get more eggs. And we didn't have nearly enough vanilla. And . . .

Okay, deep breath.

Everything was going to be fine. If I took my time, my cookies would be perfect. But before I could start baking them, I was going to need more ingredients.

I made a list and took a quick trip to the grocery store. Three other unicorns tried to stop me and talk about the party, but I didn't have time to talk! I had to get home and start baking. Two hours had already gone by.

I got home and started back at organizing my ingredients. I measured out the flour for each recipe that called for it. I used cups to hold the sugar. I got out my collection of sprinkles and decided which colors I'd use for which recipes. And then I got to work for real.

It went downhill quick.

I can pinpoint a couple of fatal flaws. Here I go.

Flour and baking soda look a lot alike. Like they look identical. Same thing with salt and sugar.

*SIDE NOTE: I remember a lesson we did in Mr. Canter's science class about how to tell them apart, but in my defense, I was making COOKIES! I wasn't in a science lab. Still, after the labels for the ingredients got "accidentally" thrown out, I wish I'd taken the time to at least taste what I thought was sugar before putting it in every recipe.

Let me tell you this. When I took the first bite of the rainbow chip cookies that were supposed to be sweet and amazing, you know what they tasted like?

SALT! It was horrible.

Then there were the chocolate clover blossom cookies. I didn't even have to taste those to know something was wrong. The second I tried to use the spatula to take them off the cookie sheet, they crumbled into a pile of greenish powder.

THEY WERE NOT EVEN COOKIES!

So my first (and second) fatal flaw(s) were accidentally using baking soda for the flour and using salt for the sugar.

The only good news here? Sugar Plum Sparkles who lives on the edge of Glitterville and has a farm has a bunch of chickens. You know what chickens like to eat?

ANYTHING!

Wait, was that much salt going to be bad for the chickens? I'd have to make sure to ask her before just giving them the remnants of my cookie disaster.

COOKIE DISASTER!

THIS WAS AWFUL!

I WAS A COMPLETE AND UTTER FAILURE AT COOKIE BAKING!

No, it was okay. I wasn't a failure. I mean I was, as far as this batch of cookies went. But for the next batch of cookies, I was going to learn from my mistakes.

I put all the messed up cookies into a pail and dropped it off with Sugar Plum Sparkles. She promised she'd take care of the salty thing and make sure my cookie rejects wouldn't hurt her chickens. Then I stopped by the store for more ingredients. An hour later I was back home, ready to try again.

That's when there was a heavy knock on the door.

Who would seriously be bothering me now? Unless it was Star, which I knew it wasn't because of how heavy the knock was, I had party business to take care of!

"Just a second!" I called, and I hurried to the door, my apron still on.

When I pulled the door open, I could not believe my eyes!

"Rotgus? Bundek?"

"Yes and yes," Rotgus said.

*SIDE NOTE: In case you don't remember, Rotgus and Bundek were my two dwarf friends who I'd gone on an adventure with to get rid of a grumpy ogre. They lived in Goldcrest, a city up north.

"What are you two doing here?" I asked.

"Doing here?" Bundek said. "What kind of greeting is that?"

"I'm sorry! Come in!" I was actually thrilled to see the dwarves. "I'm just surprised. The party's not for two days."

They both tried to step in at the same time and got stuck in the doorframe. Then Rotgus pushed ahead and stumbled in. "We didn't want to miss a second of the party!"

Bundek held up a bag. "And we brought presents for you and all your unicorn friends, care of Rotgus's wife." At this last part, he winked.

"Wife!" I said. "Congratulations!" Rotgus had been trying to prove himself to the mayor of Goldcrest, a dwarf named Arlin. I guess after helping get rid of the ogre, things had gone well.

"Yep," Rotgus said. "Arlin is sorry she couldn't come to the party, but being the mayor of Goldcrest is a full-time job."

"But we're here," Bundek said. "Now what do you need help with?"

I glanced back to all my cookie ingredients sitting on the counter. "Do you guys know how to make cookies?"

They both started laughed.

"Of course we do," Rotgus said. "Just leave this to us."

So I did. I left the two dwarves in the kitchen, and I went back to decorating. I hung the mistletoe and started on the party favors. All the while, the dwarves chatted away as delicious smells started to come from the kitchen. I tried to stay out of their way, but finally I couldn't take it anymore.

I wandered back into the kitchen. "How are the cookies?" I asked.

Bundek grinned, showing off a mouthful of thick teeth that looked like they could bite through rocks. "Take a look for yourself."

I opened the oven door with a hoof and peered inside. The rainbow chip cookies were at the perfect color of tan. I could almost imagine sinking my teeth into them right now.

"Can I have one?" I asked.

Bundek closed the oven door. "We have to wait until they're done."

"But they look done now."

"Nope," Rotgus said.

And the dwarves let another ten minutes go by before pulling the tray of cookies out.

Two things about dwarves and cookie baking:

1) Yes, dwarves did know how to bake cookies. All sorts of cookies, and they didn't even need recipes when they mixed together the ingredients. They also didn't seem to have issues with keeping the sugar and salt straight.

2) Dwarves liked their cookies burned and hard. By burned I mean the cookies were nearly black. And when I say hard, what I mean is that they want cookies that are almost like rocks.

Bundek picked up one of the cookies and bit right through it with his teeth. I winced because I was sure if I did the same, I'd break a tooth. And I had strong teeth! But he gave a thumbs up and said, "Perfect!"

I didn't like to tell other creatures how to do things, but in this case, I had to intervene.

"So here's the thing about unicorns," I said. "We like our cookies a lot less done." And I tried to explain how ten minutes ago the cookies would have been perfect.

Rotgus and Bundek of course disagreed with me, but after some serious cookie negotiation, we came to an agreement. Half the cookies would be baked "dwarf style" and half the cookies would be baked "unicorn style." But I also needed to make sure we had enough cookies, so I ran to the store and got even more ingredients. They'd have to make double the cookies I'd planned on making if we were going to have enough.

So that's how today went. Tomorrow would be last-minute preparations, and then it was on to the party!

DATE: MAGICDAY, EMERALD 18

Diary, I'm not going to spend a lot of time on today. Rotgus and Bundek were up early, making more cookies. They also decided we'd need punch, three cakes, about a million French fries, and popcorn. So yes, I went to the store for more stuff.

At least I didn't have to cook.

But given that I had so much time on my hooves, and given that my mare wasn't home, so she would never know, I decided to use a little magic to make my perfect tree look even more perfect.

THIS WAS A MISTAKE!

I could stop here and go to bed, but I owe it to you to tell you what happened. Also, it did end up really good, and I know you want to hear that part.

So I decided that I would use magic to create a rainbow glitter spray to dust the tree with. I didn't want to coat all the pine needles in glitter. Then I wouldn't be able to see them. But I also wanted to make sure there was enough glitter that all my unicorn friends would be able to see the rainbow colors.

I was sure it was going to be fine. I was sure my magic would work great.

Two things:

1) It was not fine.

2) My magic did not work great.

So I lowered my horn, and I thought magical thoughts. And yes, nothing happened. Then I doubled my magical thoughts and a small spray of purple glitter came out of my horn.

IT WAS A START!

Sure, it was nowhere near enough, but at least I knew my magic worked.

Well, at least for that brief moment it did. I tried again, but no matter what magical thoughts I tried, the magic was not coming back.

"But you did magic just great when you fought that ogre," Bundek said. "Remember?"

He was right! My magic had worked them. And the reason why? It was because . . .

Okay, I'm not sure of the exact reason why, but it had something to do with these marker stones that were scattered all over the land. They'd been put in place ages ago by unicorns to help guide travelers. I had some kind of special connection to the marker stones. Like I kind of communicated with one once, and then, when I was facing the ogre, I'd thought of the marker stone, and that's when my magic had worked.

"Just don't watch me," I said to Rotgus and Bundek. So they turned back to baking.

Then I lowered my horn and focused on my magic again. And in my mind, I pretended that a marker stone was right there in the room with me, and that the symbols on it were glowing. And I was sure I could see it and almost read the symbols. They lit up in different colors, and the stone seemed to call my name.

Then . . .

Magic burst from my horn. There was a spray of glitter that was like none I'd ever seen before, not even when Racer Diamonds had the glitter disaster that covered the entire science lab. Glitter of every color sprayed from my horn. It swirled in the air, getting everywhere.

"Stop, Shiny!" Rotgus shouted from the kitchen. I couldn't see the dwarves because the glitter was too thick. I couldn't even see the Christmas tree anymore.

I tried to pull back on the magic, but the glitter kept coming. It got in my eyes. In my mouth. I tried again to stop it. I imagined the marker stone crumbling to dust. I even thought about yelling at the imaginary marker stone.

Then the door of my house burst open.

"What is going on in here?" someone shouted.

And at the sound of the voice, my magic fizzled away.

Then a huge breeze blew through the room, like a creature (a very large creature) was blowing away dust. The glitter cleared enough for me to see where the breeze was coming from.

"Razz!" I shouted.

My dragon friend was here! He'd gotten the invitation! First the dwarves and now him. Those raccoons should start a mail service.

"Shiny, what kind of mess are you in now?" Razz boomed.

I sank to my haunches. This magic stuff was exhausting.

"I was trying to decorate my tree," I said.

"What tree?" Razz asked.

I turned to look at the tree, but it was completely covered in glitter. Like you couldn't see a single pine needle or branch or decoration.

I lifted a hoof and pointed at it. "This tree?"

Then Razz stepped into my house and blew hard at the tree. Glitter flew off it. About half the glitter went out the window and half pooled on the floor behind the tree.

"Oh, that tree," Razz said. "It's nice, but you don't have a star."

Then he pulled a shiny gold star (I'm sure it was real gold!) from a hidden spot under one of his scales and placed it on top of the tree.

It gleamed in the daylight, and the entire room brightened.

It was better than I'd ever imagined!

"You don't get to keep the star, Shiny," Razz said.

Same old Razz.

"I figured." Then I hurried over to give him a hug, but Razz held up a clawed hand.

"No hugs," he said. "Remember?"

Definitely the same old Razz.

"I'm glad you made it for the party," I said.

"Me, too, Shiny," Razz said. "Me, too."

DATE: GLITTERDAY, EMERALD 19

PARTY DAY!

In my mind I knew exactly how today was going to go.

1) Unicorns would show up on time! (Timeliness is very important.)

2) Every unicorn would remember their Secret Santa present. (I'd wrapped mine for Sassy Mane last night and hidden it away.)

3) We'd sing. We'd drink punch. We'd eat cookies (and cake and French fries). We'd open presents.

4) And when it was time for every unicorn to leave, they were all going to tell me that it was the most fun and amazing party they'd ever been to.

You know what? I didn't do bad.

Not bad at all!

Here's how the day went.

I woke up crazy early. Like the sun hadn't even popped above the horizon yet and it was so dark in the house that I had to light a few of the magic light globes around the house. The first thing I saw (okay heard . . . wait a minute. Maybe this is what woke me up) was Rotgus and Bundek asleep in front of the fire, snoring so loudly I was sure unicorns two houses away could hear. But I didn't rush over and wake them because there was something really peaceful about having the house to myself.

The second thing I saw was the counter of cookies. Or at least where the counter of cookies was supposed to be.

Yes, the counter was there.

The cookies?

THE COOKIES?

THEY WERE GONE!!!!!

And sleeping in front of the Christmas tree was Razz with cookie crumbs all over his mouth.

"YOU ATE ALL THE COOKIES!" I shouted so loud that it hurt my own ears.

It was loud enough to wake not only Razz but also Rotgus and Bundek who jumped up, knocking over a pretty red flower my mare had brought home.

"Who ate all the cookies?" Rotgus shouted.

"The dragon made me do it," Bundek said, and that's when I noticed that his beard was covered in crumbs also.

I stomped forward until I stood in the middle of Razz and Bundek. "You two stayed up after I went to bed and ate all the cookies?"

Razz licked his lips. "Maybe." He didn't look the least bit sorry.

Bundek, on the other hoof, couldn't even look me in the face. He said, "I couldn't stop myself. They were so tasty."

I put my hooves on my hips. "Well, I wouldn't know. And now no other unicorns will know either."

Bundek actually looked like he was about to cry. "I'm really sorry, Shiny."

"Eh, what's the big deal?" Razz said. "We can make more."

MAKE MORE?!?! The party was in five hours.

"We only have one oven. We don't have time," I said. This was a disaster.

But Razz started laughing. "One oven!"

"What's so funny?" I saw nothing humorous in this cookie fiasco.

"I'm an oven," Razz said, and he blew a small stream of fire out of his nostrils.

Hope began to filter back into my mind. Maybe . . .

"You can bake the cookies?" I asked.

"Sure," Razz said. "If the two dwarves make the dough, I'll bake them."

Yes! This was going to be perfect.

"But I'm still tired," Bundek said, patting his stomach. "I ate too much last night."

I glared at him. He lowered his hand from his stomach and brushed the crumbs out of his beard. "But I can sleep later. Let's get baking."

The three of them hurried over to the kitchen and got started. By now the sun had come up enough to brighten the room. I turned off the magic light globes because my mare always told me I had to conserve the magic in them so they wouldn't run out. Then I assessed the room to figure out what needed to be done.

EVERYTHING!

Sure, there was a star on top of the tree, but there were no other ornaments because they'd all been blown off when Razz got rid of the glitter. I picked a couple up off the ground, but there were so many. And the candy dishes were all empty and needed filled. I needed to put more decorations both inside and out. I had to get the music ready.

THERE WERE SO MANY THINGS TO DO :(

I needed help.

"Be right back!" I said, and I ran out the door and over to Star's house.

"Please come help me!" I said when she opened the door.

Star's face fell. "I can't Shiny. I am so sorry, but the last dress rehearsal for the play is this morning and I can't miss it."

I tried not to let the disappointment show on my face. But that's right. She'd gotten them to move the rehearsal so it wouldn't be in the middle of my party.

"Maybe you can get Dashing Hearts to help?" Star said.

I imagined Dashing Hearts, with his dark blue mane brushed to perfection, red hearts shining. I could ask him to help. But then I remembered how "helpful" he'd been when we'd gone looking for the tree.

Nope, I was not going to ask Dashing Hearts. He was probably getting his beauty sleep anyway.

"It's okay," I said. "I have a better idea. I'll see you at the party. Don't be late!"

And I trotted off, heading a couple streets over to Sassy Mane's house. When I got there, I lifted a hoof and knocked on the door. Sassy Mane's mare answered it on my third knock.

"Sassy Mane," she called. "Shiny Fluffy Hooves is here to see you."

There was some kind of grumbling that I couldn't quite make out, then finally Sassy Mane showed up at the door.

OMG!

Her aqua blue hair was pointing in every direction. Her white and aqua blue mane had tangles in it that I never would have believed possible. And her eyes were barely open because I'd obviously just woken her up.

"Hi, Sassy!" I said, trying to sound all happy. But this was stressful and what was I doing here?

"What is it, Shiny?" Sassy Mane said, yawning. "Shouldn't you be home getting ready for your party or something?"

That's when I couldn't keep the smile on my face any longer. "That's why I'm here," I said. "I still have so much to do and the dragon and one of the dwarves ate all the cookies and there's still glitter everywhere and I'm never going to be able to get all the decorating done by myself, and I really need help."

I blew out a breath when I finished because it may have been the longest sentence I'd ever spoken in my life.

Sassy Mane used a hoof to brush some of the sleep out of her eyes. "Okay, I get it, Sassy. You need help decorating. And why are you here?"

I'd thought this part was obvious, but I guess she was going to make me ask.

"Will you please come help me decorate for the party?" I said. Then I held my breath again as I waited for her answer.

Sassy Mane looked at me. I mean really looked at me. I could almost see the thoughts spinning around in her mind as she weighed her options. Then she said, "Fine. I'll help. But I need to leave at least one hour before the party starts so I can come back here and get ready. Okay?"

Was that okay?

DEFINITELY!

"That is perfect!" I said. That still gave us almost four hours to decorate.

Sassy Mane's mare made us a couple of hot sparkle lattes to bring along, and we trotted back to my house. Sassy Mane hardly said a word the entire time, and I didn't want to push my luck with random chit chat and make her change her mind.

Then we walked through the door.

"Shiny!" she said. "You really do have a dragon and two dwarves here!" She stared into the kitchen where Razz was just blowing fire on a tray of cookies.

"Well, yeah," I said. "Did you think I was lying?"

She slowly turned her head to me. "Maybe. I mean I don't know. You just have all these amazing stories, and I'm not sure which are made up and which I should believe."

"They're all real," Bundek called from the kitchen. He reached into his leather pouch and pulled out a mouse. "In fact, this is the ogre that Shiny Fluffy Hooves assisted us in catching."

Assisted! Whatever!

"Put the mouse away," I said. The last thing we needed was a mouse getting into the cookie batter.

"Ogre," Bundek called, and slipped his pet back into the leather pouch.

Sassy Mane finally pulled her eyes away from them and scanned my house. "Oh, you really do have a lot of decorating still to do."

"I told you so!" I said.

And I'll give Sassy Mane credit. We spent the next three and a half hours decorating everything, inside and out. (I made sure to keep the Secret Santa present I'd gotten for her out of sight so she wouldn't know that I was her Secret Santa.) Sassy Mane kind of took over on the decorations, but I didn't mind. She was REALLY GOOD at this stuff! And I was beyond happy for the help. And as the minutes ticked by, my house transformed from a regular unicorn house into a winter wonderland.

My mare walked out of her room and stopped in her tracks. "Oh, everything looks beautiful!"

Not just beautiful.

IT WAS PERFECT!

When it was finally time for Sassy Mane to leave so she could get ready for the party, I was almost sad to see her go.

"I couldn't have done this without you," I said.

Sassy Mane batted her gorgeous eyelashes. "I know, Shiny." Then she trotted out the door without another word.

Okay, we weren't the best of friends yet (and probably never would be—let's face it), but she had really come through when I needed her.

"And we're just about done over here, too," Rotgus said.

I'd been so busy with decorating the house that I hadn't peeked into the kitchen in the last couple hours. But when I did . . .

WOW!

Piles and piles of cookies sat in perfect stacks on the counter. Not only were there more cookies than yesterday, but they were magical. Like I'd never known so many cookie recipes could exist.

"Yeah, not bad, right," Rotgus said. "Once we realized that we could do whatever we wanted, it really gave us creative freedom."

"Here try one, Shiny," Bundek said, and he passed over a green and white stripped cookie. It melted in my mouth, and the delicious taste of peppermint filled me with joy.

"You guys are amazing, you know that, right?" I said.

"I know that," Razz said.

Of course he did. I grinned.

"Thanks, Shiny," Rotgus said. "Now let's get ready for the party!"

※ ※ ※

The first guests would be here in less than five minutes. I hurried and placed my Secret Santa present under the tree. Rotgus and Bundek put a bunch of identically wrapped presents in a pile under there. And Razz . . . He reached behind a scale to where he kept his hidden treasures, and pulled out a bunch of silver pieces.

"Not gold, Shiny," he said. "You know I don't part with my gold."

I did know that.

"You know unicorns don't use money," I said.

"Use!" Razz said. "These coins aren't to spend. They are to be admired. And kept very securely. In fact, maybe I should keep them safe." He reached forward with his claws as if he was going to swipe the whole batch back.

"Leave them, dragon," Bundek said. "Once you give a present, you can't take it back. That's bad luck."

"Oh!" Razz said. And the bad luck comment must have gotten to him because he pulled his claws back and left the pile of silver where it was.

Star was the first to arrive, and she was beyond herself when she met Razz.

"A real dragon!" she said, and she reached out a hoof. "Can I touch one of your scales?"

Razz eyed her, like he was sure she was trying to steal all his treasure.

"This is my best friend," I said, and that seemed enough to appease him.

He turned to the side and let Star touch a scale. Her eyes went wide. "Dragons are the coolest creatures in the world!" she said. And from that moment on, they were inseparable.

Of all unicorns, Sassy Mane got there next, looking amazing and not at all like she'd spent the morning helping me decorate. She placed two presents under the tree.

"Two?" I said.

She kind of shrugged. "One for my Secret Santa and one for you." Then she leaned close. "But this doesn't mean we're friends."

A PRESENT FOR ME!

"Of course not," I said. What an awkward conversation. Thankfully I was taken away from it when Bruno the Guardian of Maps arrived with Sweet Cupcakes and Old Gray Stars. All the other unicorns started to arrive also. And with every unicorn that stepped through my door, my heart was filled with joy.

Dashing Hearts was one of the last to arrive. Sure, he looked amazing, with his mane braided and tied with beads and ribbons. He walked in and stood there like he was waiting for me to compliment him.

When I didn't, he said, "How do I look?"

SERIOUSLY?

"Fine," I said.

His smile faltered just a bit. Then he looked up.

"Oh, mistletoe!" Dashing Hearts said. And he leaned forward like he was going to kiss me under the mistletoe.

NO WAY!!!

I can't believe a week ago I would have gone all swoony to be in this spot. But right now, first off, I didn't want to kiss any unicorn under the mistletoe, and second off, I certainly didn't want to kiss Dashing Hearts.

I stepped back. "Presents go there, and cookies and snacks are on the counter." Then I dashed away as quickly as I could without bumping into any other unicorns.

* * *

Yes, I was totally nervous for the Secret Santa present swap. What if Sassy Mane hated my gift? But when she opened it, the smile that lit up her face was like I'd never seen before. Okay, sure, she quickly hid it and looked at me.

I made a motion with my hoof across my mouth like I wasn't going to say a word. Then she put the constellation hair accessory in her mane.

Who was my Secret Santa? Mr. Canter, our science teacher! This normally might not seem like a very cool thing to have your science teacher bring you a present, but he got me a really official looking lab coat and a glass beaker. Sure there was a list included also of all the substances I shouldn't mix together, but I could read that later.

Rotgus and Bundek gave every unicorn (and Bruno and Razz) a lucky rock.

BRUNO IMMEDIATELY ATE HIS!

"Double the luck," Bruno said. "And now I'll never forget to keep it with me."

The dwarves actually thought this was hilarious, and they latched onto Bruno and kept asking him to eat pebbles and stones and the hard "dwarf style" Christmas cookies.

Old Gray Stars fell asleep in the middle of everything, at the kitchen counter on an empty cookie platter.

I opened the present from Sassy Mane which was a coupon for one hour of her time teaching me how to put on makeup and style my hair. I realized this implied that I was doing it all wrong, but I was in way too good of a mood to get offended.

Racer Diamonds tried to get up the nerve to kiss Star under the mistletoe, but the most he could bring himself to do was give her a friendly hoof-shake.

Finally the sun started to set. The party had to end.

From the front door, Sassy Mane called, "Quick, you all, come outside. It's about to happen."

Every unicorn rushed to the door. No sooner had I stepped out onto the nice grass in my front yard, the entire sky lit up.

I tilted my head upward and saw the most amazing sight. A shooting star shot across the dark night sky. Silence filled the party, and we all looked up together. There was this weird, mystical moment where I felt like we were all connected. And I'm pretty sure it was the most magical moment I'd ever experienced.

After the shooting star vanished, back to wherever it came from, my guests started to leave.

Sassy Mane came up to me and whispered in my ear. "I really liked the present."

I smiled. "I thought you would."

Then she left and so did every other unicorn except Star.

Rotgus and Bundek brought out the rest of the cookies, and we sat with Razz and the dwarves under the stars until it was finally midnight.

<u>MERRY CHRISTMAS, TO EVERY CREATURE EVERYWHERE!</u>

ABOUT THE AUTHOR

Connor Hoover thinks unicorns are real and is determined to get a picture to prove it. She's pretty sure there's one living in her backyard right now. Connor lives in Austin, Texas with two tortoises, two dogs (and possibly one unicorn), and takes pictures of rainbows every chance she gets.

To contact Connor:
connor@connorhoover.com
www.connorhoover.com

Made in United States
Orlando, FL
08 November 2021